LET'S INVESTIGATE

Ratio
and Proportion

LET'S INVESTIGATE
Ratio and Proportion

By Marion Smoothey
Illustrated by Ann Baum

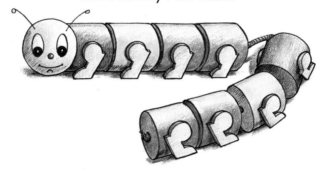

MARSHALL CAVENDISH
NEW YORK • LONDON • TORONTO • SYDNEY

© Marshall Cavendish Corporation 1995

Published by Marshall Cavendish Corporation
2415 Jerusalem Avenue
PO Box 587
North Bellmore
New York 11710

Series created by Graham Beehag Book Design

Editorial consultant: Prof. Sonia Helton
University of South Florida, St. Petersburg

Library of Congress Cataloging-in-Publication Data

Smoothey, Marion,
  Ratio and Proportion / by Marion Smoothey; illustrated by Ann Baum.
    p. cm.. — (Let's Investigate)
  Includes index.
  ISBN 1-85435-776-X ISBN 1-85435-773-5 (set)
  1. Ratio and Proportion — Juvenile literature. [1. Ratio and
Proportion.] I. Baum, Ann ill. II. Title.
  III. Series: Smoothey, Marion, 1943- Let's Investigate.
QA117.S64 1994   94-17995
513.2'4—-dc20   CIP
                              AC

Printed in Malaysia by Times Offset (M) SDN BHD

Contents

This book will help you to find the answers to problems about finding fair shares and comparing sizes and amounts of similar objects, quantities, and groups.

You will need a ruler to measure some of the drawings and you will find it helpful to have a basic calculator.

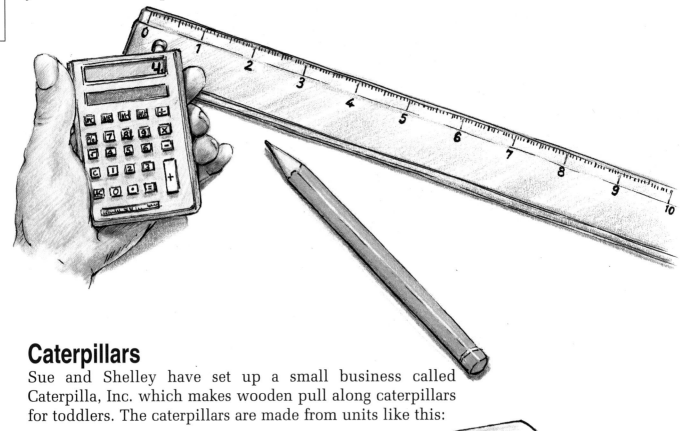

Caterpillars

Sue and Shelley have set up a small business called Caterpilla, Inc. which makes wooden pull along caterpillars for toddlers. The caterpillars are made from units like this:

The segments are painted different colors and threaded on a string. The caterpillars are assembled in different color combinations. Each color combination is given a different head and a name so that children can collect the whole set.

This is the collection.

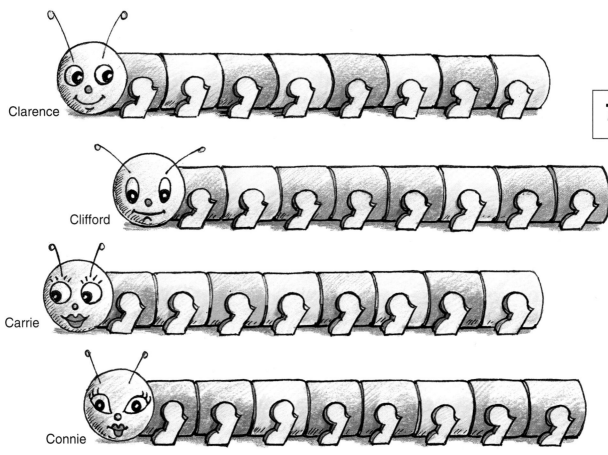

Clarence

Clifford

Carrie

Connie

When Sue and Shelley receive an order from a shop, they have to calculate how many segments of each color they will need and how many heads.

● **1.** How many red segments do they need to make one Clarence?

● **2.** How many yellow segments do they need to make a Connie?

Check your answers to page 7 on page 62.

This is an order from Little Rascals Preschool.

8

● **1.** What color segments do they need for this order?

● **2.** How many segments do they need all together?

● **3**. How many segments do they need of each color?

● **4.** What segments do Sue and Shelley need to make a complete set of caterpillars?

Sue and Shelley find that they have 12 red segments and 12 yellow segments in stock. They can make either three Clarences or two Connies.

● **1.** If they make two Connies, how many yellow segments will be left over?

● **2.** What caterpillars can they make from these segments?

● **3.** What heads have to go with these segments?

Here are the quantities of segments for the whole set of caterpillars.

					Total
Clarence	4 red	4 yellow			8
Clifford	2 red	2 yellow	4 blue		8
Carrie	2 red	4 yellow	1 blue	1 green	8
Connie	6 red	2 yellow			8
	14 red	12 yellow	5 blue	1 green	32

● **1.** How many heads do they need for a set?

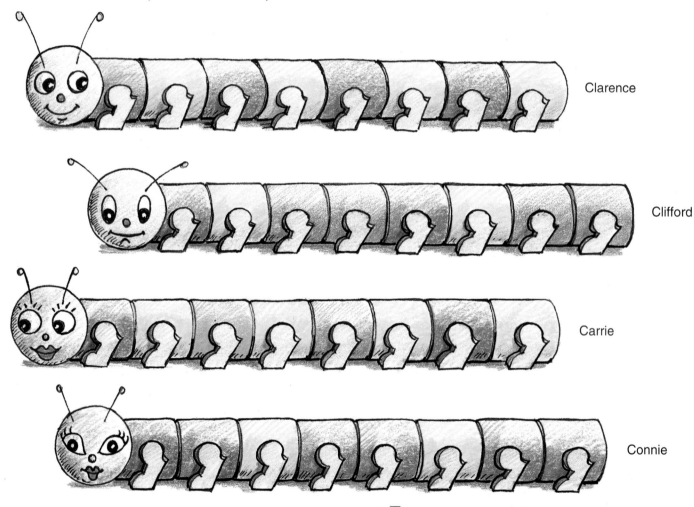

Clarence

Clifford

Carrie

Connie

● 1. What caterpillars will these segments make? How many caterpillars will there be?

● 2. What other segments do you need to make these segments into Connies?

● 3. What heads do you need to go with these segments?

Horrible Hag's Hotpot

12

Horrible Hag is having five of her friends over to lunch and has decided to serve her favorite recipe.

Hotpot
Serves 12
the diced tails of 12 snakes
18 black skinned moldy carrots
6 large rotten squishy onions
8 large green potatoes thinly sliced
      with a few slivers of finger
10 cups of stagnant pond water
      a little black mud to thicken
1 tbsp. chopped dandelion leaves for garnish
salt and pepper to taste

Horrible Hag is puzzled. She has only four potatoes that are green enough to use.

● **1.** How should she change her recipe to serve six?

Knitting Patterns

Pat designs and machine knits sweaters in various colors and patterns. Cloudy Day uses ten balls of blue wool, three balls of white, two of green and one of brown.

● **1.** She has an order for 20 Cloudy Day sweaters. How much white wool does she need?

This is the amount of green wool left in stock after completing the order.

● **2.** How many more Cloudy Day sweaters can Pat make?

The Ratio Sign

Clarence and Connie are made from the same kind of red and yellow segments but they are different from each other because the ratio (*raysheeo*) of red to yellow segments is different.

Clarence has one yellow for every red segment. The ratio of yellow to red segments is 1 : 1. 1 : 1 is said as ``one to one.'' The symbol : is used as a sign for the ratio of one thing to another.

Clarence

Connie

Connie has one yellow for every three red segments. The ratio of yellow to red segments is 1 : 3 (one to three).

The order of the numbers is important. The order of the numbers has to be the same as the order of the words.

If you mix blue and red paint in the ratio of 5 : 2, it means that for every five measures of blue paint, you use two measures of red paint. This will give you seven measures of dark purple paint.

If you mix blue and red paint in the ratio of 2 : 5, it means that for every two measures of blue paint, you use five measures of red paint. This will make seven measures of a brighter purple paint.

Ratios of More than Two Groups

Horrible Hag's hotpot recipe had several ingredients. Each of them can be expressed as a ratio of any of the others. The ratio of potatoes to pond water to snake tails is 8 : 10 : 12 (eight to ten to twelve).

It does not matter that the potatoes are counted as individual items and the water is measured in cups. It is the ratio between them that is important.

If Horrible Hag wants to make enough for six people instead of twelve, she halves all the quantities. If she is holding the Hags' Annual Dinner for 120, she will have to multiply all the quantities in the recipe by ten.

In Pat's knitting pattern for the Cloudy Day sweater, the ratio of blue to white to green to brown wool is 10 : 3 : 2 : 1 (ten to three to two to one). If you change the order of the colors, you must change the order of the numbers to correspond.

The ratio of green to blue to white wool is 2 : 10 : 3.

● **1.** What is the ratio of brown to white to green wool in the Cloudy Day pattern? Write your answer using the ratio sign.

● **2.** In a Carrie caterpillar, what is the ratio of red to yellow to green to blue segments?

MATCHING RATIOS

● Match these ratios to the correct drawings.

A. Lions to lionesses: 1 : 4, 2 : 5, 3 : 2.

B. Lionesses to lions: 5 : 1, 3 : 2, 1 : 4.

C. Chairs to tables: 6 : 1, 5 : 3, 2 : 4.

D. Tables to chairs: 1 : 3, 2 : 4, 6 :1.

16

1.

2.

3.

4.

5.

6.

Check your answers on the next page.

Check your answers to pages 16 and 17 before you try the next page

A.

5. Lions to lionesses 1 : 4

3. Lions to lionesses 2 : 5

6. Lions to lionesses 3 : 2

B.

1. Lionesses to lions 5 : 1

4. Lionesses to lions 3 : 2

2. Lionesses to lions 1 : 4

C.

4. Chairs to table 6 : 1

3. Chairs to tables 5 : 3

2. Chairs to tables 2 : 4

1. Table to chairs 1 : 3

6. Tables to chairs 2 : 4

5. Tables to chair 6 : 1

● Now try these.
A. Ducks to drakes to ducklings 1 : 1 : 3, 2 : 1 : 5
B. Drakes to ducks to ducklings 1 : 1 : 2, 2 : 1 : 3
C. Ducklings to ducks to drakes 3 : 2 : 2, 1 : 3 : 1

The Same Ratios

Ali is painting his bedroom purple. He mixed the shade himself from six cans of blue and four cans of red. Now he has run out of paint and has to mix some more of the same shade.

Ali must use blue and red cans in the same ratio as his original mixture. Otherwise he will get a different shade of purple

● **1.** Which of these cans are in the same ratio as Ali's original mixture and will make the same shade of purple?

● **2.** Ali has only one can of red and two cans of blue left. How can he finish off his room with the matching shade of purple?

Seals and Fish

The zookeeper must feed the seals in the ratio of five fish to one seal at each feeding time to keep the seals in good condition.

● He has just fed them. Has he done his job properly? Assume that the seals have not yet eaten any of the fish!

Tops, Legs, and Screws

Tabpak is a firm that supplies bulk packs of tops, legs, and screws for hotels and restaurants to assemble into tables. The tops, legs, and screws should be in the ratio 1 : 4 : 12.

● Which of these packing lists is incorrect?

1.
SCREWS 120
LEGS 50

2.
SCREWS 144
LEGS 48
TOPS 12

3.
SCREWS 60
LEGS 20
TOPS 5

SCREWS 94
LEGS 32
TOPS 10

4.
TOPS 8

Ratios in Their Simplest Form

Tiling

24

Inez is tiling her kitchen floor in a pattern of blue and white tiles. Each tile is one foot square. The kitchen measures 20 feet long and 16 feet wide.

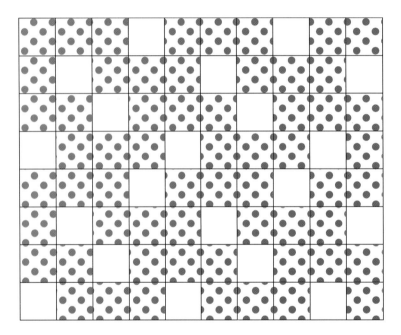

● **1.** How many blue tiles does Inez need to cover the whole floor?

● **2.** How many white tiles does she need?

You could say that the ratio of blue tiles to white tiles is 60 : 20, but this is not the simplest way of expressing the ratio. If you look more closely at the pattern you can see that it is made by repeating and turning a block of four tiles.

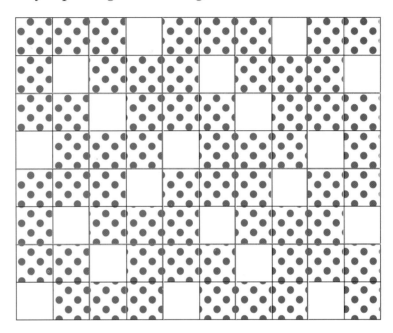

Look again at the caterpillar collection on page 7.

The simplest way of expressing the ratio of blue to white tiles is 3 : 1. "*Simplest*" used in this way means "the smallest complete group that can be separated out and repeated."

To make a Clarence, Sue and Shelley need four red segments and four yellow, so you can say the ratio of red to yellow segments is 4 : 4. If you look more closely, however, you can see that the segments can be divided into four pairs.

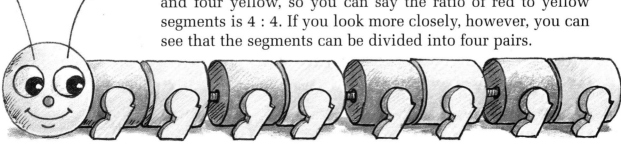

Each segment has one red and yellow segment. The simplest ratio of red to yellow segments in a Clarence is 1 : 1.

Connie is a little more difficult. She needs six red and two yellow segments. But if you look carefully, you can split her into two matching groups.

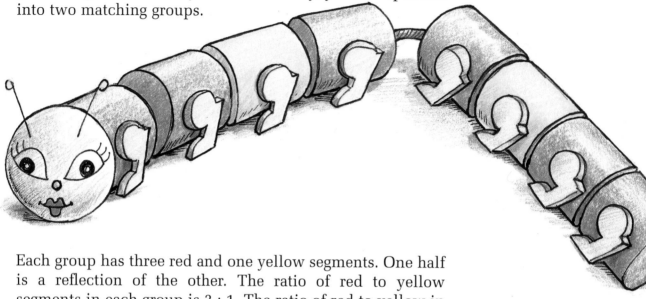

Each group has three red and one yellow segments. One half is a reflection of the other. The ratio of red to yellow segments in each group is 3 : 1. The ratio of red to yellow in a Connie is 3 : 1.

● **1.** What is the simplest ratio of yellow to red segments in a Connie? (Be careful – it isn't 3 : 1!)

● **2.** What is ratio of red to yellow to blue segments in a Clifford?

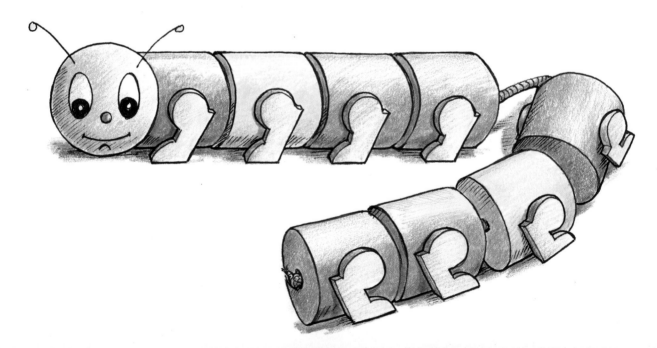

Kites

Express in the *simplest* form the ratio of green to orange bows in these kite tails. Use the ratio sign.

Party Favors

David and his mother are preparing bags of party favors for his birthday party guests. These are the contents.

Give your answers in the *simplest* form.

- **1.** What is the ratio of candies to noisemakers?
- **2.** What is the ratio of marbles to pens to balloons?
- **3.** What is the ratio of balloons to candies to pens?
- **4.** How many candies go with each balloon?
- **5.** What is the maximum number of guests for whom David and his mother can make matching party favors?
- **6.** What will each bag contain?

ANSWERS TO PAGE 19

1.

A. 1 : 1 : 3

2.

A. 2 : 1 : 5

3.

B. 1 : 1 : 2

4.

B. 2 : 1 : 3

C. 3 : 2 : 2

5.

6.

C. 1 : 3 : 1

Ratios and Groups

When you were looking at the kite tails, it was easy to divide the bows up into groups in order to find the simplest ratios.

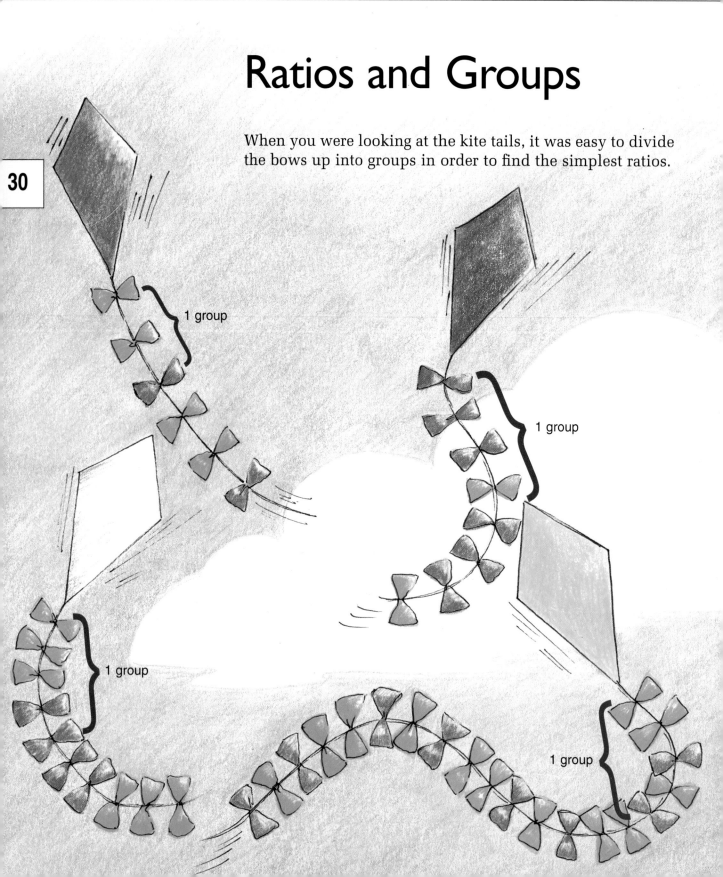

● **1.** In their simplest form and using the ratio sign, what are the ratios of blue to white tiles in these patterns?

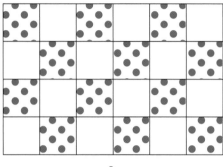

A.

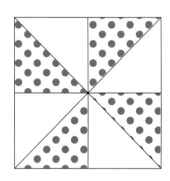

C.

B.

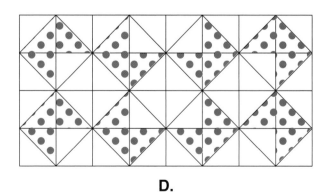

D.

E.

In all the tiling patterns on pages 30 and 31, it is possible to figure out the ratios of blue to white tiles by breaking each of the patterns down into a smaller group, or block of tiles, which is repeated to make the pattern.

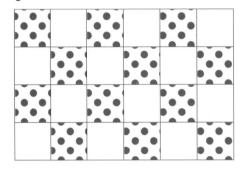

Pattern A is made by repeating a block of two tiles, one blue and one white.

In the second and fourth lines of the pattern the block is **rotated** 180 degrees. Each block is made of one blue and one white tile. The ratio of blue to white tiles in pattern A is 1 : 1.

In pattern B, the basic block that makes the pattern is two blue tiles and one white tile.

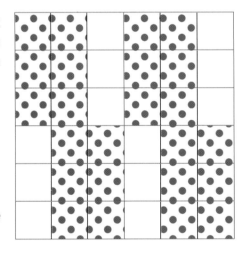

The ratio of blue to white tiles is 2 : 1.

The tiles in pattern C are a different shape: they are triangles instead of squares. You can still pick out the basic block that makes the pattern. It is one blue triangle and one white triangle. The ratio of blue to white tiles is 1 :1.

The basic block for pattern D is a square made up of eight small triangular tiles. In each square block, three of the triangular tiles are blue and five are white. The ratio of blue to white tiles is 3 : 5.

 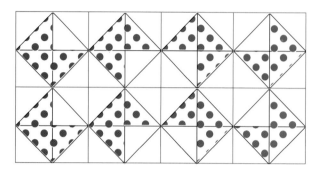

In E, the basic block is a rectangle made up of four triangles. Each rectangular block has three blue triangles and one white one. The ratio of blue to white tiles is 3 : 1.

Calculating Ratios

It is not always easy to figure out ratios in their simplest form by looking for patterns. The idea of breaking a pattern down into smaller blocks only works if the pattern can be completely filled with the small blocks.

In this diagram, the pattern is made from triangles, but you cannot combine the triangles in any way to completely fill the pattern with the same shape block.

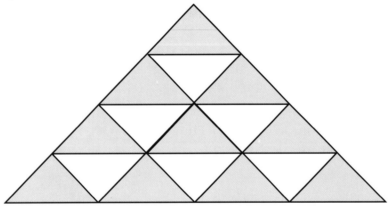

● **1.** What happens if you try to fill the pattern with a block of one white and one blue triangle like this?

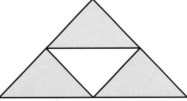

● **2.** Try filling the patterns with a block of one white and three blue triangles. Does it work?

● **3.** Experiment with blocks of your own.

Check your answers on page 36.

The easiest way to work out the ratio in this case is to total all the blue and all the white tiles. This gives the result of ten blue and six white small triangles in the large triangle.

To say that the ratio of blue to white tiles is 10 : 6 does NOT give the ratio in its simplest form.

You can see why not if the tiles are arranged like this.

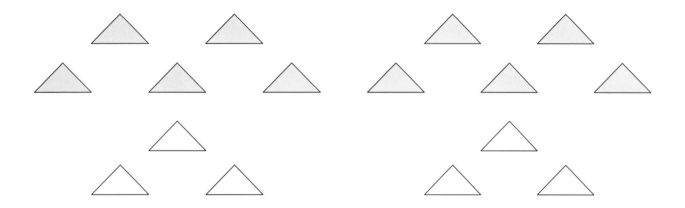

You can see that there are two equal groups of tiles. Each group has five blue and three white tiles. The ratio of blue to white tiles in its simplest form in the original pattern is 5 : 3.

Answers to page 34

1. If you use a block of one white and one blue triangle, there will be four blue triangles that have no white tiles to go with them. This is one way of showing what happens.

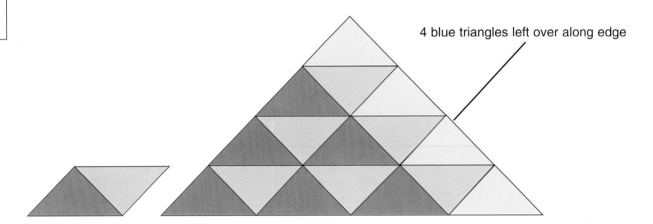

4 blue triangles left over along edge

2. If you fill the pattern with a block of one white and three blue triangles like this, you are left with a block of one blue and three white tiles in the middle of the pattern.

3 white, 1 blue triangles left over in middle

3. This is one way of splitting the pattern into two blocks that contain the same numbers of blue and white tiles, but the blocks are not the same shape.

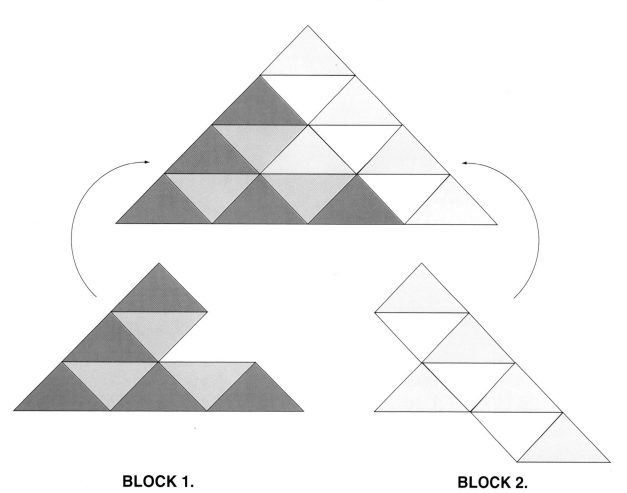

BLOCK 1.   **BLOCK 2.**

- **A.** How many blue and white tiles does each block contain?

- **B.** What is the ratio of blue to white tiles in the original pattern?

- **C.** What is the ratio of white to blue tiles in the original pattern?

Using Factors

There is a faster way of calculating the simplest ratio, and it will always work.
The triangle tiling pattern has ten blue and six white tiles.

10 and 6 can both be divided exactly by 2. We say that 2 is a common **factor** of 10 and of 6.
To find the simplest ratio of ten blue and six white tiles, divide each number by the their common factor 2.

$10 \div 2 = 5 \quad 6 \div 2 = 3$

This gives the answer that the simplest ratio of blue to white tiles is 5 : 3.

This method works for all numbers. If there is no common factor except 1, the ratio is already in its simplest form
Which of these ratios are already in their simplest form?
● **1.** 2 : 5 ● **2.** 3 : 4 ● **3.** 3 : 6 ● **4.** 2 : 10 ● **5.** 3 : 5?

What are the common factors of these ratios?
● **6.** 3 : 9 ● **7.** 10 : 5 ● **8.** 14 : 21 ● **9.** 2 : 8 ● **10.** 2 : 6 : 10

A useful hint is that if there is a 1 in the ratio, then it must be in its simplest form.

The segments needed for a Carrie are two red, four yellow, one green and one blue.

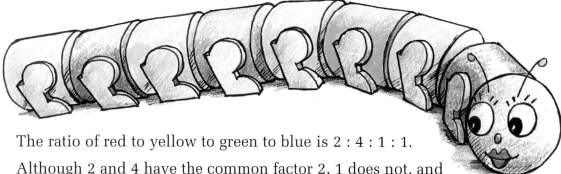

The ratio of red to yellow to green to blue is 2 : 4 : 1 : 1.

Although 2 and 4 have the common factor 2, 1 does not, and the ratio is in its simplest form already.

The balls of wool needed for a Cloudy Day sweater are in the ratio of 10 : 3 : 2 : 1. These numbers have no common factor and there is a 1 among them. This is the simplest ratio.

Anita makes necklaces like this.

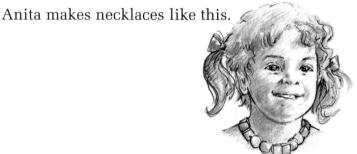

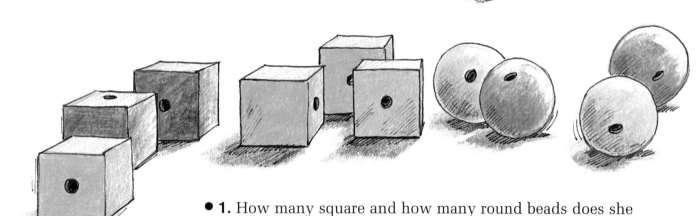

● **1.** How many square and how many round beads does she use in each one?

● **2.** What is the common factor of the number of square and the number of round beads?

● **3.** What is the ratio of square to round beads in its simplest form?

Check your answers to questions 1 to 3 on Page 63 before you try the rest of the questions

Express these ratios in their simplest form.
● **4.** 5 : 15 (What is their common factor?)
● **5.** 3 : 9 : 3
● **6.** 12 : 16 : 4
● **7.** 1 : 5 : 10
● **8.** 2 : 4 : 7

Sharing

You can use ratios to help you to solve some problems about sharing.

Problem

John and Cindy buy a candy bar between them. The bar costs 80 cents. John pays 60 cents; Cindy pays 20 cents. They agree to share the bar in the same ratio.

How much does each get of the bar?

Solution

The ratio is 60 : 20. 60 and 20 have the common factor of 20. The simplest ratio is 3 : 1.

John gets three shares for each one share that Cindy gets.

They will have to divide the bar into four equal shares. John will have three of the four shares, and Cindy will have one.

Note that you have to add the ratios together to find the total number of shares in which to divide up the bar.

Try these:

● **1.** Tina is 12 and Andrew is 8. They clean out the garage for their mother. She gives them 10 dollars and says they must share the money in the same ratio as their ages.
How much do they each get?

● **2.** There is four times as much nitrogen as oxygen in air. How much nitrogen is there in 20 gallons of air?

● **3.** Concrete can be made from cement powder and sand in the ratio of 2 : 5.
How much sand does it take to make 35 pounds of drymix? (Drymix is the mixture of sand and cement powder before water is added.)

● **4.** The Beenes, the Chases, and the Douglases rent a vacation cabin for 11 weeks. The Beenes use it for 14 days, the Chases for 35, and the Douglases for 28. They agree to split the total cost of $3,300 in the same ratio as the length of time they have used the cabin.
How much does each family pay?

Check your answers on page 43.

More sharing problems

● **1.** Sally and Gary help Mrs. Roberts get her garden ready for spring. Sally works for six hours and Gary for five hours. Mrs. Roberts pays them $44. They agree to split the money in the same ratio as the hours they worked.
How much do they each receive?

● **2.** Water has twice as much hydrogen as oxygen.
How much oxygen is there in 60 gallons of water?

● **3.** An alloy contains copper, tin, and zinc in the ratio 5 : 2 : 3.
How much tin is needed to make 30 tons of alloy?

● **4.** When Sue and Shelley set up Caterpilla, Inc., Sue invested $800 and Shelley $700. They agreed to share the profits in the same ratio.
How much do they each get from a profit of $3,000?

Check your answers on page 47.

Answers to page 41

1. The ratio of 12 : 8 in its simplest form is 3 : 2. (The common factor is 4.)

Tina gets three shares; Andrew gets two shares.

There are five shares all together. (3 + 2 = 5)

Each share is worth $2. ($10 ÷ 5 = $2)

Tina gets $6; Andrew gets $4. (3 × $2 = $6; 2 × $2 = $4)
Check: $6 + $4 = $10, which was the amount to be shared.

2. The ratio of nitrogen to oxygen in air is 4 : 1.

There are five shares all together. (4 + 1= 5) For 20 gallons, each share is worth 4 gallons. (20 gallon ÷ 5 = 4 gallons)

Every 20 gallons of air contains 16 gallons of nitrogen. (4 × 4 gallons)

3. The ratio of powder to sand is 2 : 5.

There are seven shares all together. (2 + 5 = 7)

For 35 pounds, each share is worth 5 pounds. (35 lb ÷ 7 = 5 lbs.)

It takes 25 pounds of sand to make 35 pounds of concrete. (5 × 5lbs. = 25 lbs.)

4. First you must change the days to weeks.

The ratio of weeks is 2 : 5 : 4. The only common factor is 1. This is the simplest ratio.

Check that the shares total 11 weeks. (2 + 5 + 4 = 11)

Each share is worth $300. ($3,300 ÷ 11 = $300)

The Beenes pay $600. (2 × $300 = $600)

The Chases pay $1,500. (5 × $300 = 1,500)

The Douglases pay $1,200. (4 × $300 = $1,200)

Check: $600 + $1,500 + $1,200 = $3,300.

43

If you did not figure out the correct answers to the
questions on page 41, turn back to page 42

Similar Figures

44

These figures are congruent. They are exactly the same shape and the
same size.

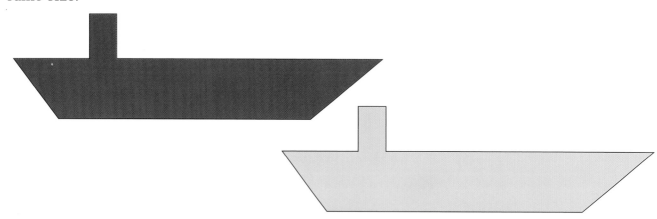

These figures are similar. They are the same shape but different sizes.

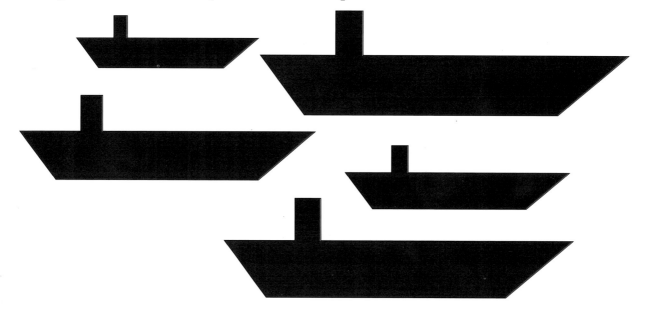

These figures are not similar. the outline is made up of the same pieces; each ship has one funnel, a hull, a bow, and a stern, but they are not in the same proportion. The ships look as if they have been stretched or squashed compared to the original.

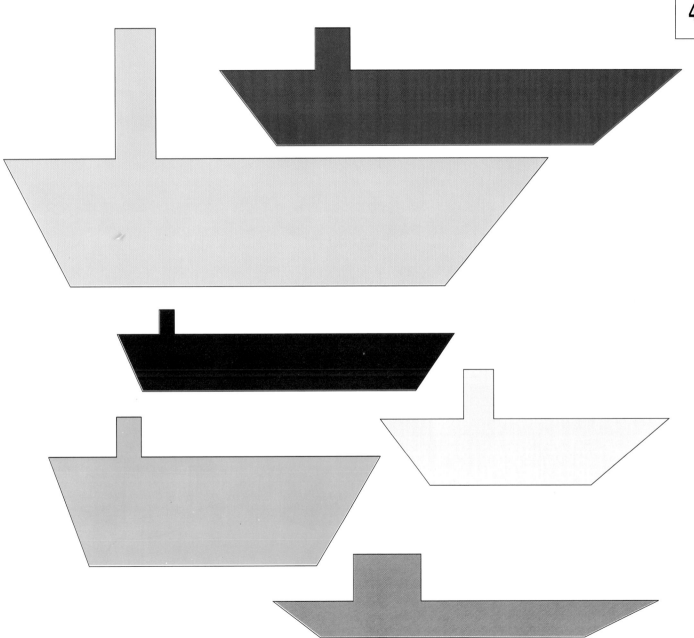

● Which of these trees are similar?

1.

2.

3.

4.

5.

6.

7.

8.

Answers to page 42

1. The ratio of hours worked is 6 : 5. This gives a total of 11 shares. Each share is worth $4 ($44 ÷ 11 = $4).
Sally earns 6 × $4 = $24; Gary earns 5 × $4 = $20.
Check: $24 + $20 = $44.

2. The ratio of hydrogen to oxygen in water is 2 : 1. This gives a total of 3 shares. For 60 gallons of water, each share is worth 20 gallons (60 gallons ÷ 3 = 20 gallons).
Every 60 gallons of water contains 20 gallons of oxygen.

3. The ratio is 5 : 2 : 3, so the total shares are 10
(5 + 2 + 3 = 10).
To make 30 tons of alloy, each share is worth 3 tons
(30 tons ÷ 10 = 3 tons).
6 tons of tin are needed to make 30 tons of alloy
(3 tons × 2 = 6 tons).

4. The ratio is 800 to 700. The total shares are 1,500.
Each share is worth $2 ($3,000 × 1,500 = $2).
Sue gets $1,600 and Shelley $1,400.
Check: $1,600 + $1,400 = $3,000.

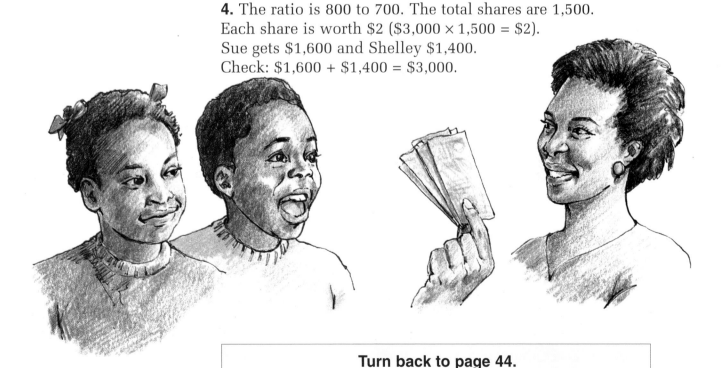

Turn back to page 44.

Investigating Ratio

It can sometimes be difficult to judge whether or not two figures are similar just by looking at them. You can make sure by measuring matching parts of each figure.

Copy this table.

48

LENGTH	RED SHIP	YELLOW SHIP	RATIO OF RED TO YELLOW IN SIMPLEST FORM
A			
B			
C			
D			
E			

Use a ruler to measure accurately the lengths marked on the similar red and yellow ships opposite. Enter the results in your copy of the table.

When you have a half in your answer, you may need to double it to find the simplest ratio. For example, if you have measurements of 3½" and 7", the simplest ratio is 1 : 2.

You can look at it two ways. The quick way is to say 7 is twice as big as 3½. Or you can double to get 7 and 14; the common factor is 7. The simplest ratio is 1 : 2.

● What do you notice about your results in the last column of the table?

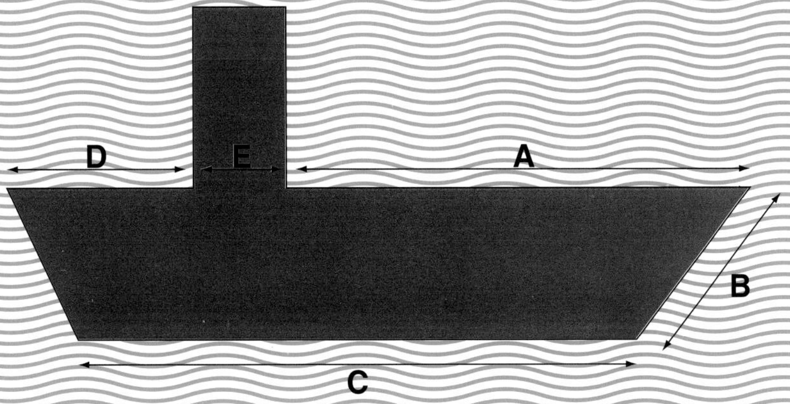
D
E
A
B
C

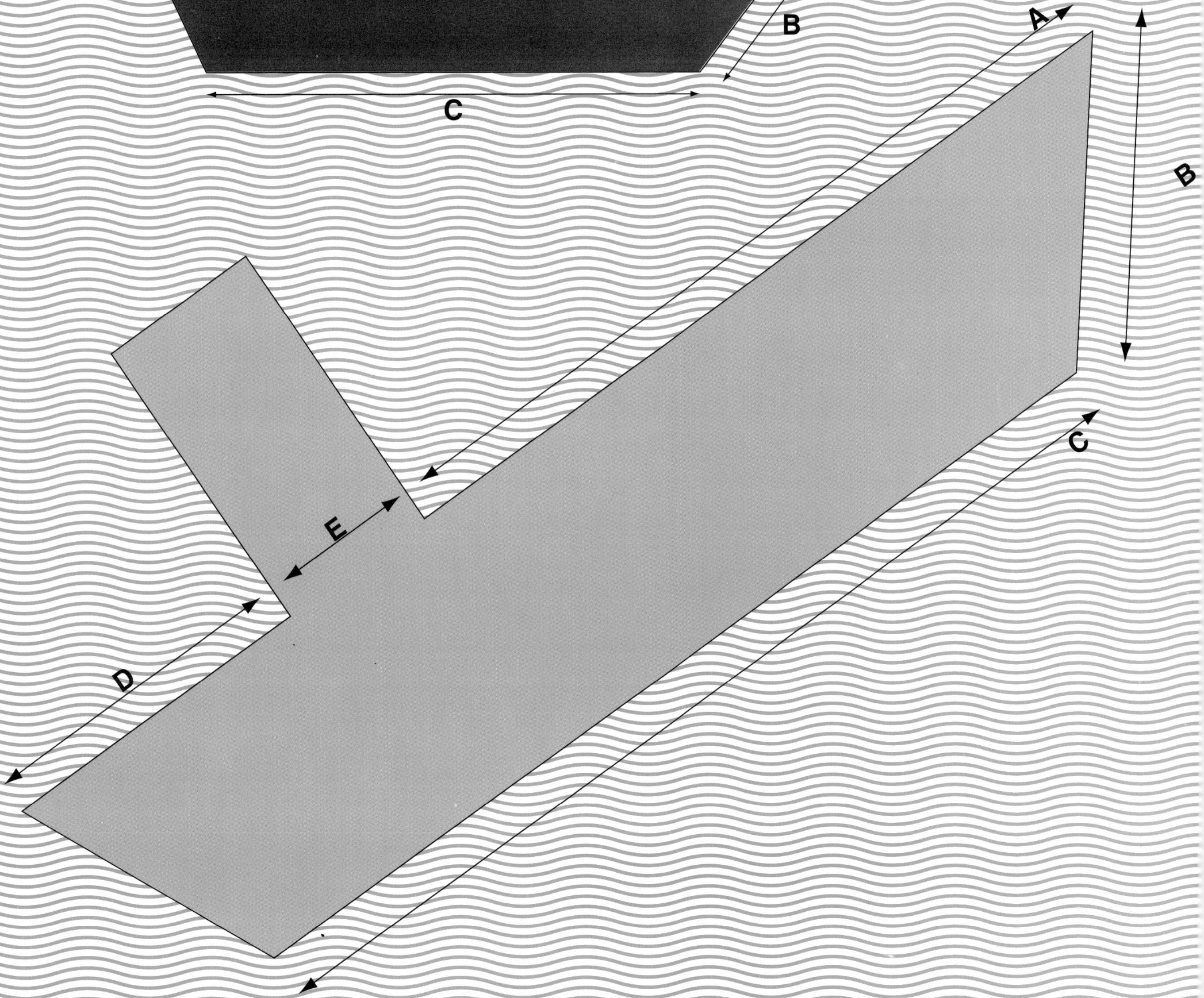
A
B
C
E
D

Your table should look like this.

LENGTH	RED SHIP	YELLOW SHIP	RATIO OF RED TO YELLOW IN SIMPLEST FORM
A	$2\frac{1}{2}$	5	1 : 2
B	1	2	1 : 2
C	3	6	1 : 2
D	1	2	1 : 2
E	$\frac{1}{2}$	1	1 : 2

You can see that the ratio of the lengths of matching parts of the similar red and yellow ships is always the same 1 : 2.

Check the rest of the matching parts to see if they are in the ratio 1 : 2.

When figures are similar, each part of them is in the same ratio.

You can use this fact to find unknown dimensions

Example

An artist wishes to paint an accurate copy of this Peacock butterfly. She wants to make it an enlargement so that the painting can be seen better. She decides to make the wing-span of the painted butterfly 7½". (The wing-span is the distance from one wing tip to the other at the widest point.)

1"

An enlargement is a similar figure. The ratio of each part of it to each matching part of the original figure must be the same.

The ratio between the lengths of the hulls of the red and yellow ships is the same as the ratio between the widths of their funnels or the ratio between the lengths of their decks. Whichever pair of parts you choose, the ratio remains the same.

If the painting is to be an exact enlargement, the ratio of each part of the original butterfly to its partner on the painting must stay the same.

● **1.** Measure the wing-span of the butterfly.

● **2.** What is the ratio between the wing-span of the butterfly and the length A?

● **3.** A ratio of 2½ : 1 is the same as 7½ : ? What is the missing number?

● **4.** What length must the artist paint the body and antennae together to make the painting accurate?

Artists often use a grid to scale a drawing. The example below shows that it is fairly easy to reproduce the illustration accurately by watching carefully the shape in each square as you draw it.

Investigating Proportion

52

These rectangles are similar.

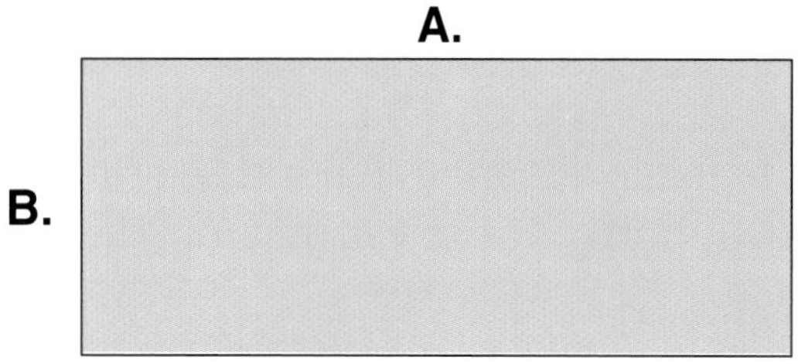

A.

B.

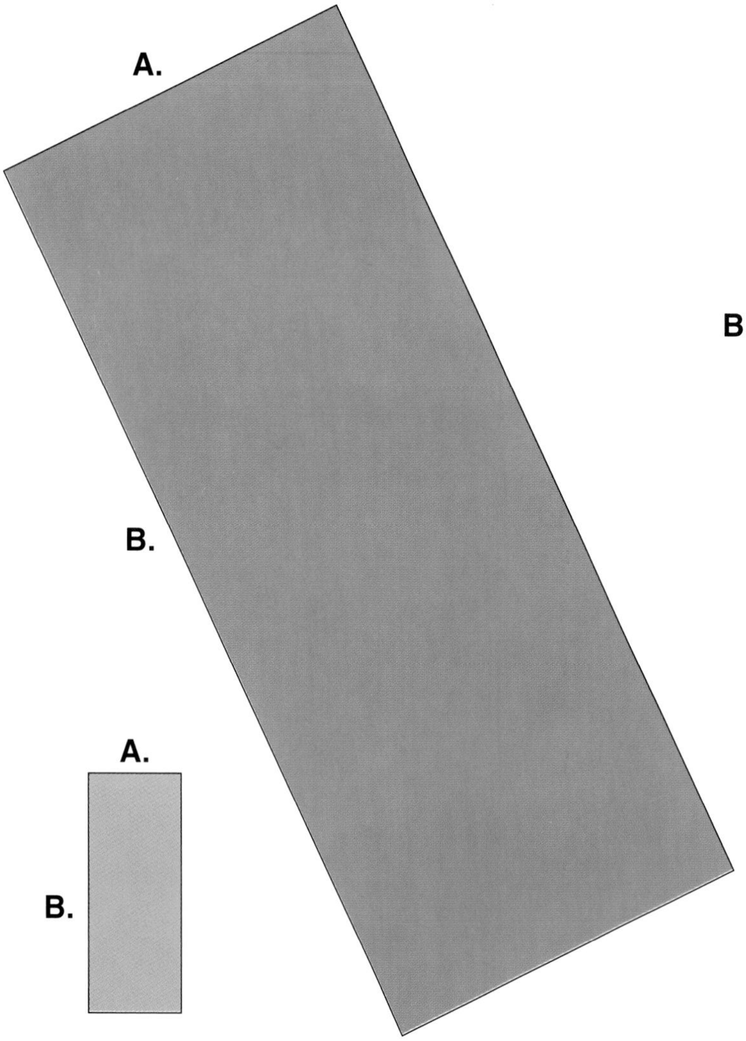

A.

B.

A.

B.

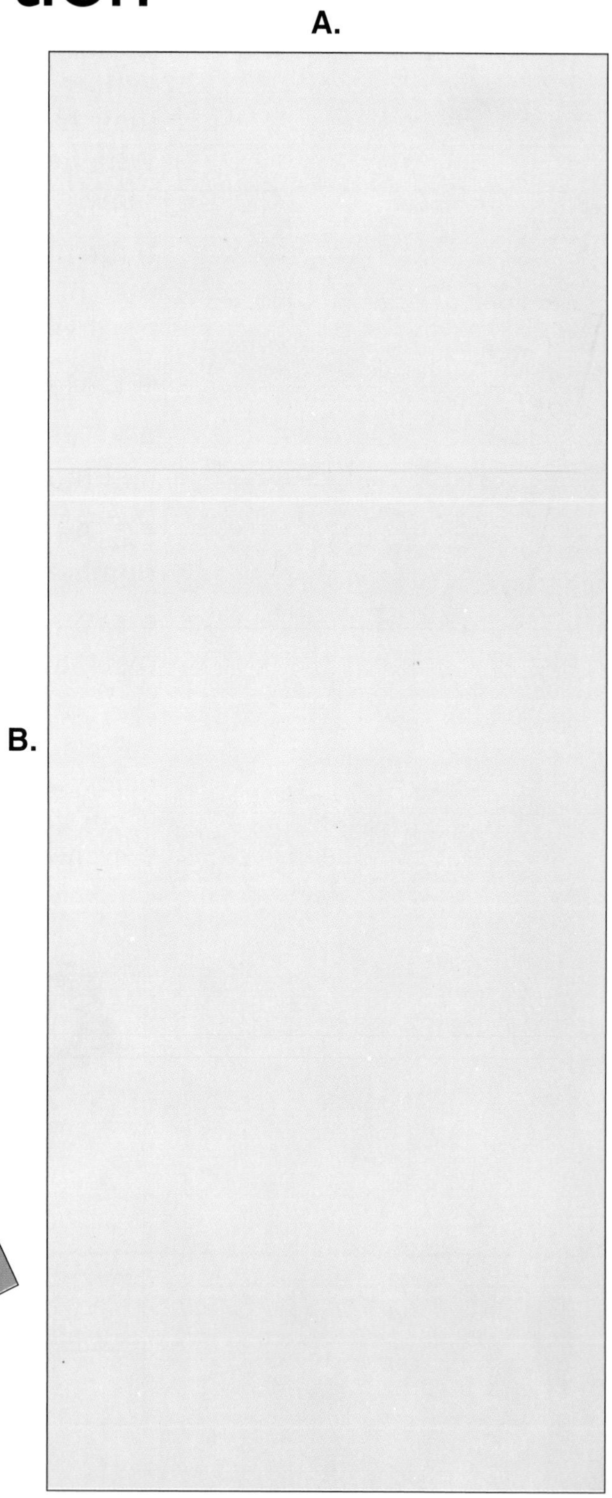

A.

B.

Make a copy of this table.

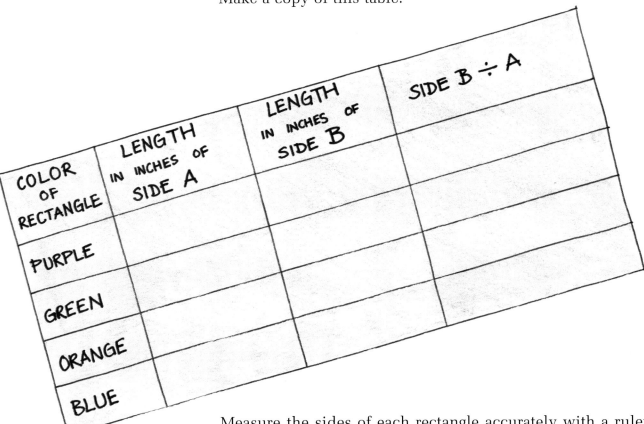

COLOR OF RECTANGLE	LENGTH IN INCHES OF SIDE A	LENGTH IN INCHES OF SIDE B	SIDE B ÷ A
PURPLE			
GREEN			
ORANGE			
BLUE			

Measure the sides of each rectangle accurately with a ruler and enter the results in your copy of the table. If you find it difficult to divide fractions, change them to decimals and use a calculator.

$$\frac{1}{2} = 0.5 \qquad \frac{1}{4} = 0.25$$

● What do you notice about your results in the final column of the table?

Your table should look like this:

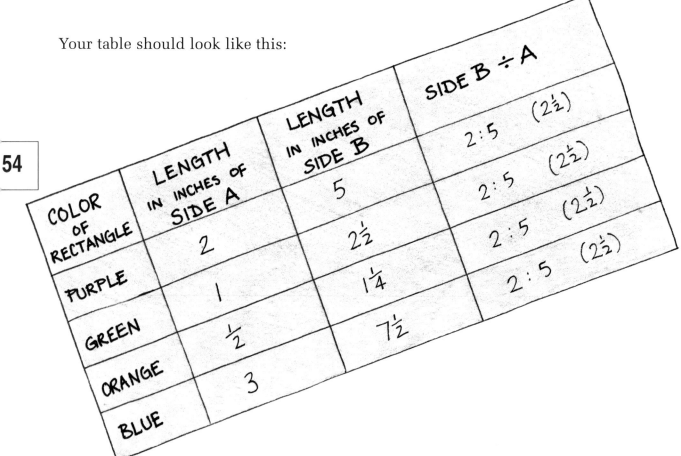

COLOR OF RECTANGLE	LENGTH IN INCHES OF SIDE A	LENGTH IN INCHES OF SIDE B	SIDE B ÷ A
PURPLE	2	5	2 : 5 $(2\frac{1}{2})$
GREEN	1	$2\frac{1}{2}$	2 : 5 $(2\frac{1}{2})$
ORANGE	$\frac{1}{2}$	$1\frac{1}{4}$	2 : 5 $(2\frac{1}{2})$
BLUE	3	$7\frac{1}{2}$	2 : 5 $(2\frac{1}{2})$

You can see that in each rectangle,
    the long side ÷ the short side = 2.5.

This is the proportion of the long side to the short side.

In each of the rectangles,
    the long side = $2\frac{1}{2}$ × short side.

The proportion of the short side to the long side is 0.4 or $\frac{2}{5}$ (short side ÷ long side × 0.4).

In each of the rectangles,
    short side 0.4 (or $\frac{2}{5}$) × long side.

> **Figures that are similar have matching pairs of lengths in the same proportion.**

You can use this fact to check whether or not figures are similar.

Finding Similar Figures by Proportion

Measure the long and short sides of each of these rectangles:

A.

A.

(b)

B.

B.

Calculate the proportion of the short to the long side of each of the rectangles.

If you wish to use a calculator, change 1½ to 1.5 and 3¾ to 3.75.

● **1.** Which rectangle is similar to those on pages 52 and 53?

Check your answer on page 63 before you attempt the next section

Measure the height and width (at the widest point) of this fish.

● **2.** What is the proportion of height to width of the fish?

● **3.** What is the proportion of width to height of the fish?

● Which of these pictures are of the same fish as the one you measured on the previous page? Remember if they are pictures of the same fish they must be in the same proportion.

56

Finding Missing Lengths By Proportion

This picture of the fish shown on page 55 is too long to fit on the page. How long is it?

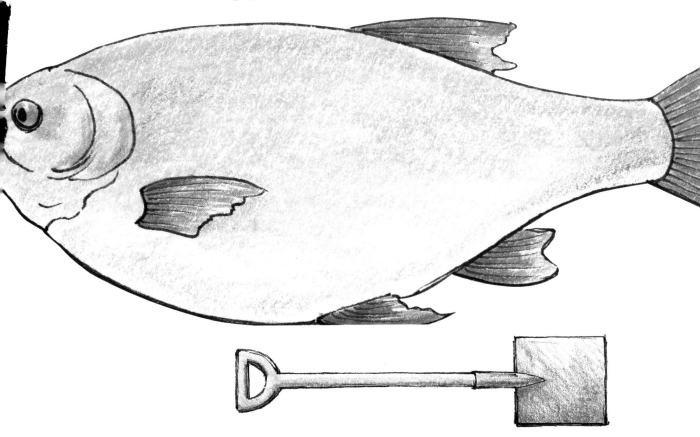

The length of the handle of this spade is 24″. The length of the spade blade is 8″.

The handle = 3 × the blade.

The blade = ⅓ × the handle.

The proportion of the handle to the blade = 3

The proportion of the blade to the handle = ⅓

58

● **1.** Which of these are pictures of the same spade as the one on page 57?

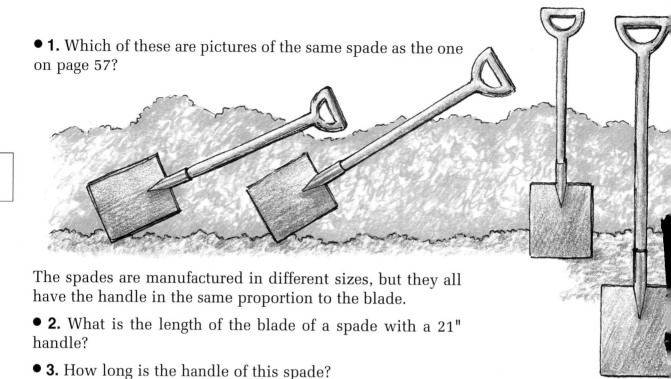

The spades are manufactured in different sizes, but they all have the handle in the same proportion to the blade.

● **2.** What is the length of the blade of a spade with a 21" handle?

● **3.** How long is the handle of this spade?

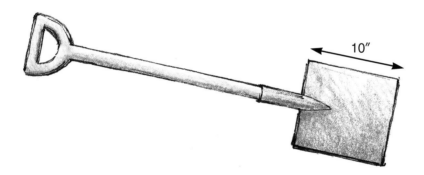

10"

● **4.** How long is the blade of this spade, and how long is the handle?

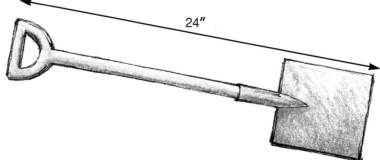

24"

● **5.** What is the total length of a spade with a 27" handle?

The bicycles of the 1870's had large front wheels and small back ones. Usually the ratio of the diameter of the front wheel to the diameter of the back was about 2 : 1.

This is a picture of one of these early bicycles.

Neck

● **1.** The diameter of the front wheel of the bicycle shown in the drawing was 50", What is the diameter of the rear wheel?

● **2.** What was the height of the front wheel?

Measure the base of the soda bottle in the drawing and its height from the base to the neck.

● **3.** Calculate the proportion of the base diameter to the height.

● **4.** The diameter of the base of the soda bottle which is in the same proportions as the one in the drawing is 7". What is its height?

● **5.** The soda bottle's total height is 33". What is the diameter of its top?

Don't Get Caught

Not all problems that concern the relationship of one thing to another can be solved by ratio or proportion. Sometimes you have to think twice and use your common sense.

Examples

If 3 men dig a hole 5 feet square and 3 feet deep in 2 hours, how long will 6 men take to dig the hole?

It is tempting to answer 1 hour, but 6 men could not work in a hole that small.

Eva weighs 126 pounds when she is 16. How much will she weigh when she is 48?

It is silly to say she will weigh 3 times as much when she is 3 times as old. Weight and age are not in proportion once we are fully grown.

Glossary

alloy a mixture of metals

circumference the distance around the edge of a circle

congruent the same shape and size; identical

diameter the distance through the center of a circle from one point on the circumference to another point on the circumference

dimension a measurement such as length, height, depth, or thickness

enlargement an exact copy on a larger scale

factor a number that divides exactly into another number; 1, 2, 3, 4, 6, and 12 are factors of 12; 5, 7, 8, 9 10, and 11 and any number greater than 12 are not factors of 12.

proportion the number of times one dimension is multiplied to produce another. In a triangle with a base of 3" and a height of 6" the proportion of the height to the base is 2. The proportion of the base to the height is $\frac{1}{2}$.

ratio means the same as proportion but is expressed in a different form. In a triangle with a base of 3" and a height of 6" the ratio of the height to the base is 2 : 1. The ratio of the base to the height is 1 : 2.

reflection a mirror image

rotate turn; a rotation of 180º is a half turn

similar shapes are similar when their proportions are the same but their sizes differ

Answers

Page 7
1. They need four red segments for each Clarence.
2. They need two yellow segments for each Connie.

Page 8
1. They need red and yellow segments.
2. They need 40 segments all together (5 × 48).

3.

			Total
1 Connie	6 red	2 yellow	8
4 Clarences	16 red	16 yellow	32
	22 red	18 yellow	40

4. See page 10.

Page 9
1. Eight yellow segments will be left over.
2. Two Carries can be made.
3. Four Clifford heads are needed.

Page 10
1. They need four heads for a set.

Page 11
1. You can make five Carries.
2. You need 48 red segments. These will make eight Connies.
3. You need four Clifford heads.

Page 12
Halve the quantities of each of the ingredients.

Page 13
1. Pat needs 60 balls of white wool.

2. She has enough green wool for three sweaters.

Page 15
1. 1 : 3 : 2
2. 2 : 4 : 1 : 1

Pages 16 & 17
See page 18

Page 19
See page 29

Pages 20 & 21
3, 4, and 6 are in the same ratio.
7. Ali can use 1½ cans of the blue and 1 can of the red.

Page 22
The keeper has not done his job properly. Groups 1, 2, and 4 have the correct ratio of seals to fish; groups 3, 5 and, 6 do not.

Page 23
Packing list **1.** Should have 40 legs.
Packing list **4.** Should have 96 screws.

Page 24
1. 60 blue tiles
2. 20 white tiles

Page 26
1. 1 : 3 2. 1 : 1 : 2

Page 27
1. 2 : 1
2. 1 : 3
3. 3 : 2
4. 3 : 2

Page 28
1. 4 : 1
2. 3 : 1 : 2

3. 2 : 4 : 1
4. Two candies go with each balloon.
5. The maximum number of complete bags is ten.
6. Each bag contains one noisemaker, four candies, one pen, two balloons, and three marbles.

Page 30
See pages 32-33

Page 37
A. Each block contains five blue and three white tiles.
B. The ratio of blue to white tiles in the original pattern is 5 : 3.
C. The ratio of white to blue tiles in the original pattern is 3 : 5.

Page 38
1, 2, and **5** are in their simplest form.
6. Common factor 3.
7. Common factor 5.
8. Common factor 7.
9. Common factor 2.
10. Common factor 2.

Page 39
1. Anita uses six square and four round beads for each necklace.
2. The common factor is 2.
3. The ratio of square to round beads in its simplest form is 3 : 2.
4. 1 : 3 (common factor of 5)
5. 1 : 3 : 1 (common factor of 3)
6. 3 : 4 : 1 (common factor of 4)
7. 1 : 5 : 10 (no common factor except 1)
8. 2 : 4 : 7 (no common factor except 1)

Page 46
1, 2, 4, and 6 are similar. 5 and 8 are different shapes. 3 and 7 have different details.

Pages 48 & 49
See page 50

Page 51
1. The wing-span measures $2\frac{1}{2}$".
2. $2\frac{1}{2}$: 1
3. $2\frac{1}{2}$: 1 is the same as $7\frac{1}{2}$ to 3.
4. 3"

Page 53
See page 54

Page 55
1. (b) is similar to the rectangles on pages 52 & 53.
2. The height of the fish is 3 × 4 the width.
3. The width of the fish is $\frac{1}{3}$× 4 the height.

Page 56
2, 6, 8

Page 57
The complete picture of the fish is 9" long.

Page 58
1. 2 is the same spade as the one on page 57.
2. 7"
3. 30"
4. The blade is 6"; the handle is 18".
5. 36"

Page 59
1. 25"
2. 50"
3. The base diameter is $\frac{1}{3}$ of the height to the neck
4. 21"
5. 3" ($\frac{1}{11}$ of 33")

Index